# CONTENTS

NIGERIA, CAMEROON, AND THE CENTRAL AFRICAN REPUBLIC

BY LYDIA ANDERSON

FRANKLIN WATTS
New York | London | Toronto | Sydney | 1981
A FIRST BOOK

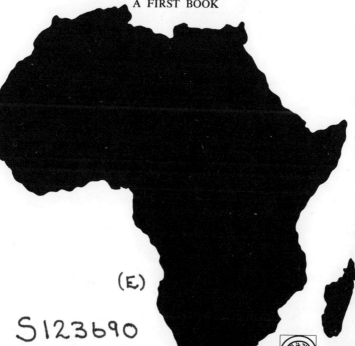

(E)

A GROLIER COMPANY

For my father, who has been
an inspiration to us all.

Cover design by Jackie Schuman

Photographs courtesy of:
Georg Gerster/Photo Researchers, Inc.: pp. 13, 47;
WHO photo by J. Mohr: p. 18;
Diane Rawson/Photo Researchers, Inc.: p. 23;
United Press International: p. 34;
Hector R. Acebes/Photo Researchers, Inc.: p. 39;
Stan Schroeder/Animals Animals: p. 42;
United Nations: p. 58.

Maps courtesy of Vantage Art, Inc.

Library of Congress Cataloging in Publication Data

Anderson, Lydia.
Nigeria, Cameroon, and
the Central African Republic.

(A First book)
Bibliography: p.
Includes index.
SUMMARY: Covers the land, wildlife,
people, languages, religion, history, economy,
health, education, and culture of three
countries of sub-Saharan Africa.
1. Nigeria—Juvenile literature.
2. Cameroon—Juvenile literature.
3. Central African Republic—Juvenile literature.
[1. Nigeria. 2. Cameroon.
3. Central African Republic] I. Title.
DT515.A765   967   80–23042
ISBN 0–531–04276–6

NIGERIA, CAMEROON, AND THE CENTRAL AFRICAN REPUBLIC

WESTERN SAHARA

CAPE VERDE

SENEGAL

GAMBIA

GUINEA BISSAU

SIERRA LEONE

LIBERIA

MAURITANIA

MALI

UPPER VOLTA

GUINEA

IVORY COAST

GHANA

TOGO

BENIN

NIGER

NIGERIA

CHAD

SUDAN

DJIBOUTI

CAMEROON

CENTRAL AFRICAN REPUBLIC

ETHIOPIA

SOMALIA

EQUATORIAL GUINEA

SAO TOME & PRINCIPE

GABON

CONGO

ZAIRE

RWANDA

BURUNDI

UGANDA

KENYA

TANZANIA

SEYCHEL

ANGOLA

ZAMBIA

MALAWI

MOZAMBIQUE

COMORO ISLANDS

NAMIBIA

ZIMBABWE

BOTSWANA

MADAGASCAR

MAURIT

REUN

SWAZILAND

LESOTHO

SOUTH AFRICA

Africa

1

AFRICA:
A MIGHTY CONTINENT

Africa is a huge continent. Only Asia is bigger. It covers 11.6 million square miles (30.2 million sq km). Parts of Africa, the lands along the Mediterranean Sea, have been in contact with people of other continents since ancient times. Around 3000 B.C., a great civilization arose in Egypt. Spreading from its kingdom along the Nile, it influenced the growth of other great cultures around the Mediterranean: the Minoan of Crete, the Greeks, and the Romans. Trade and conquest extended these empires to the shores of North Africa. The countries along the coast, as far west as the Atlantic Ocean (including present-day Morocco, Algeria, Tunisia, and Libya), remained in touch with European civilization as it advanced.

To the south, however, was the mightiest desert in the world, the vast sun-drenched Sahara. Stretching 1,200 miles (1,930 km) from north to south and 3,000 miles (4,830 km) from coast to coast, it covers an area of 3½ million square miles (9 million sq km). The entire United States could fit within its boundaries.

[1]

Long ago, in prehistoric times, the land we now know as the Sahara was covered with fertile grasslands. People lived there, hunting wild animals and gathering food and, later, herding domestic animals and growing crops. As the weather changed and the area turned from grassland to desert, these people moved southward, fleeing the desert and seeking fertile land.

Nearly all the people of sub-Saharan Africa are black, or contain characteristics of the Negroid race. Yet, as there are in all races, there are many variations among them. West African Negroes (also called Guinea Coast, Forest, or "true" Negroes) have broad flat noses, thick turned-out lips, and dark kinky hair. The Bantu, named for the language they speak, are often lighter in color, shorter in stature, with less flat noses, and thinner lips. People of the east, around the Nile Valley, are tall and slender, with thin lips and narrow noses. Pygmies and Bushmen have different features still.

Adventurous Arab traders from the east and Berbers from the north trekked in camel caravans across the dry and dusty sands of the Sahara to trade with African people on its southern borders. But, Europeans were neither encouraged nor anxious to follow.

As a result, sub-Saharan Africa (also called Tropical or Black Africa), the lands and peoples south of the Sahara, remained for centuries largely unknown to Europeans and outside the mainstream of world progress.

Sailing around the Sahara

Through their contact with traders along the Mediterranean, Europeans learned with wonder of the treasures which came from south of the Sahara. There was ivory and ebony and ostrich feathers and finely worked leather and succulent dates and bitter kola nuts and pepper and *gold*. The Europeans yearned to find the source of these exotic goods and to learn more about the "Africs" who supplied them. They also wanted to avoid the high prices charged by Arab middlemen for the precious jewels, silks, and spices they brought from the East, beyond the Red Sea. Finally, most Europeans were Christians. They didn't like dealing with the Muslim Arabs and Berbers of North Africa.

The Europeans sought to bypass the Sahara by sailing south along the western coast of Africa. But, their ships were small and, sailing before the wind, they were afraid they might not be able to return safely home. Lacking proper instruments, they feared they might lose their way. The coastline itself was forbidding and good harbors were scarce.

At length, as their ships became bigger, their sails stronger, their maps more accurate, and their instruments more reliable, they ventured farther and farther south. The Portuguese came first. Encouraged by Prince Henry the Navigator, brother of their king, they rounded the western bulge or "hump" of the continent and headed south along the coast, reaching the mouth of the Zaire (Congo) River in 1482.

By the turn of the century they had established hundreds of forts and trading posts, which they called factories, along the west coast. The "factories" handled the most lucrative commodity of all: slaves.

The Slave Trade
Slavery was common throughout most of the ancient world. Many peoples, including Africans, made slaves of defeated

enemies. Slaves were a feature of the trans-Saharan Arab trade. But, by the 1300s, slavery had almost disappeared in Europe. The Portuguese revived the trade and took Africans back to Europe, in small numbers at first, to work in Portugal and Spain.

The settlement of the New World in the sixteenth century gave rise to the expansion of this monstrous trade. Sugar plantations in the West Indies and, later, coffee, tobacco, sugar, rice, and cotton plantations in the American colonies required sturdy workers who could survive long hours of heavy labor under a broiling sun. The first shipment of slaves arrived in Virginia in 1619.

The Dutch, British, Scandinavians, and French followed the Portuguese into Africa. The slave trade grew as more and more colonies were founded in the western hemisphere. The French operated around the mouth of the Senegal River; the Dutch and British along the Gold Coast and the Slave Coast, as it came to be known, from the Gambia River to the Niger Delta.

For four centuries, slave raiders combed the coast of Africa and destroyed entire populations with a brutality unknown to the world before or since.

As many as fifteen million slaves were delivered into slavery in the Americas, to work under conditions of untold hardship far from home. Millions more died in slave raids or on forced marches to the coast or on the Atlantic crossing, chained and crowded together on slave ships without proper food, water, or fresh air.

Colonial Rule

Britain outlawed the evil slave trade in 1807, partly because it was cruel and unjust, partly because it was no longer profitable.

Other nations followed. As slavery declined, Europeans sought new sources of income for their African trade: first, through the export of minerals and raw materials, such as palm oil; later, through the development of African markets for their goods. The competition for materials and markets led to a mad scramble to control the interior of this vast continent.

Few Europeans had ventured inland before. Tangled swamps and lagoons, dense rain forest, heat, humidity, insects, and disease kept them near the shore. Besides, Africans along the coast had been happy to conduct the slave trade for them. They bartered with the powerful African chiefs of the interior for their war prisoners. Then they delivered them to the Europeans, in exchange for the cloth and tools and liquor and firearms which they hoped would make them rich and powerful, too.

Ancient Empires

Europeans called Africa the "dark" or unknown continent. Few of them realized that great African cultures had existed for centuries in the lands between the Sahara and the sea and in the south and east of Africa as well. Within the West African bulge, the kingdoms of Ghana, Mali, and Songhai established trade empires whose magnificence astonished the Arabs. They had highly organized systems of government, well-equipped armies, widespread trade, and splendid centers of learning and art.

Impressive kingdoms still flourished in the Sudan—the grassy plain which stretches between the Sahara and the equatorial rain forest—when the Europeans began to visit the continent: Kanem-Bornu, in the region around Lake Chad, and powerful Hausa states north of the Niger River. The Yoruba had developed a rich culture at Ife, near Ibadan.

Still, many Europeans thought of Africans as superstitious

[5]

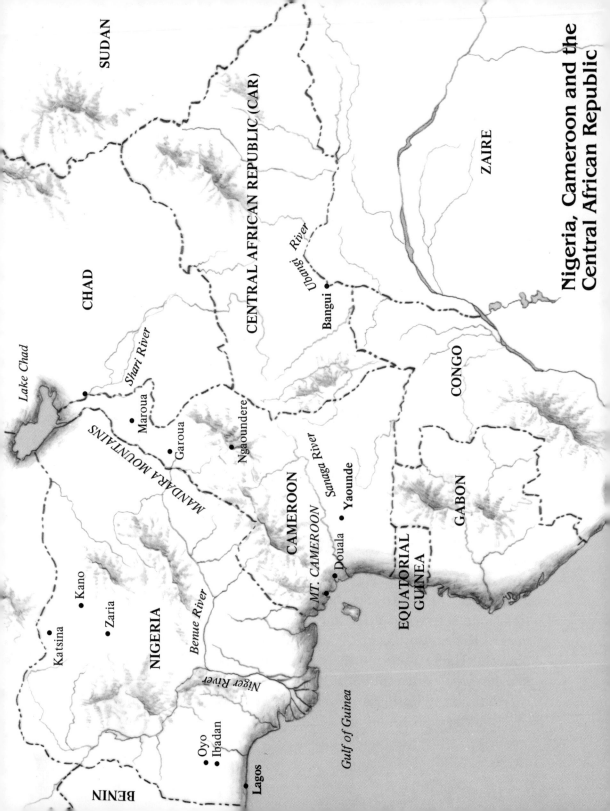

Nigeria, Cameroon and the
Central African Republic

SUDAN

CHAD

CENTRAL AFRICAN REPUBLIC (CAR)

ZAIRE

Ubangi River

Bangui

CONGO

Lake Chad

Shari River

Maroua

Garoua

Ngaoundere

MANDARA MOUNTAINS

Sanaga River

CAMEROON

Yaounde

GABON

Kano

Zaria

MT. CAMEROON

Douala

EQUATORIAL
GUINEA

Katsina

NIGERIA

Benue River

Niger River

Oyo
Ibadan

Lagos

Gulf of Guinea

BENIN

"heathens," ignorant savages, even cannibals. Of course, this helped to justify their taking them as slaves and, later, annexing their lands as colonies.

By the end of the nineteenth century, all Africa was split into colonial "spheres of influence," with no regard for the traditional boundaries of the people. In 1885, the major European powers met in Berlin, cut up the continent like a giant jigsaw puzzle, and divided the pieces. They soon subdued the African inhabitants and began to rule for their own benefit.

Explorers and Missionaries

A number of fearless explorers helped to open up the continent for the Europeans. Among them were the Scotsman Mungo Park, who explored the Niger River; David Livingston, who lost contact with the outside world for six years while he explored central Africa; and Henry Morton Stanley, the newspaper correspondent who was sent to find Livingston. Some were motivated by a concern for the well-being of the Africans and were considered by some to be heroes of the colonial era.

Missionaries representing the Christian churches of Europe wanted to help the African people, too. Park and Livingston were missionaries as well as explorers. They came to help end the slave trade. They stayed to establish schools and hospitals and to give advice on improved farming methods and nutrition and sanitation and to spread scientific and industrial knowledge: to bring Africa back into the mainstream of world progress.

Independence

Africa struggled under colonial rule for nearly a century. Then, after World War II, the cry for independence arose all over the continent. In 1950, there were only three independent nations

[7]

in all of Africa: Egypt; Ethiopia; and Liberia, a nation founded in 1847 by former American slaves. By 1980, however, almost all were free of foreign domination.

Nigeria, Cameroon, and the Central African Republic are three of the seventeen nations which achieved independence in 1960. They share the common background of sub-Saharan Africa. Yet, each has its own problems and special strengths and its own unique heritage.

2
NIGERIA

Nigeria is the richest and most influential country in black Africa today. It is also the most heavily populated: 90 million people live there—nearly three times as many as live in any other black African nation. There are more black people in Nigeria than in any other country of the world. (The United States is fourth with 24 million.)

Nigeria's wealth is based on oil. Over two million barrels of oil are produced in a day, making Nigeria the world's sixth largest producer of oil and providing the major source of the government's funds. Except for Saudi Arabia, it is the largest supplier of oil to the United States.

Nigeria is a land of contrasts as modern progress confronts age-old traditions: an oil-rich country that has a per capita income of $600; a high proportion of university graduates and a literacy rate of 25 percent. Western influence is strong in the cities; traditional values prevail in the country. Young men in leather shoes ride motorbikes and carry transistor radios; others, in loose flowing robes and colorful turbans, go barefoot. Individual achievement is highly regarded by some Nigerians and scorned by others.

Impressive government buildings rise above mud huts with thatched or corrugated tin roofs. People live in high-rise apartments and rural compounds. There are Christian missions in the south, Muslim mosques in the north, and spirits which dwell in nature everywhere.

Development of its resources has brought problems to Nigeria as everyone seeks to share the benefits of a growing economy. People have left their rural homes and crowded into the cities in search of jobs, creating unemployment there. There hasn't been enough food to go around. The cost of living has increased as much as 30 percent a year. Transportation facilities have been strained beyond capacity and corruption has existed on a wide scale.

Friction between ethnic groups and geographical areas, as well as religious differences, has prolonged the struggle for national unity. A bloody and brutal civil war broke out in 1967 and raged for thirty months when the Ibo of southeast Nigeria attempted to form the independent state of Biafra.

A military government ruled the country until October of 1979. The civilian government which assumed power faced the problem of encouraging further economic development and unifying the country when many Nigerians still prefer the old ways and feel they owe their first loyalty to their own family and ethnic group.

A VARIED LAND

Nigeria is home to 25 percent of all sub-Saharan black Africans. Population density averages 250 people per square mile

(97 per sq km), compared to 58 per square mile (17 per sq km) in the United States.

The country is 357,000 miles square (925,000 sq km). Its neighbors are Benin (Dahomey) on the west, Niger on the north, and Chad and Cameroon on the east. A low coastline, 10 to 60 miles (16 to 97 km) wide, runs for 475 miles (760 km) along the Gulf of Guinea and forms its southern border.

The coast is hot and humid and thick with mangrove swamps dotted with beautiful beaches and swaying palm trees. Lagoons provide busy ports for Nigeria's thriving trade.

Beyond the coast, running inland for 50 to 100 miles (80 to 160 km) is the rain forest. Mahogany and ebony trees grow as high as 120 feet (36 m). Lesser trees grow close together and form a canopy which allows little sunlight to reach the forest floor. Cocoa and kola trees, and rubber plantations have replaced much of the natural rain forest.

A high plateau of open woodland and savanna covers central Nigeria. Scrub and semidesert (the *Sahel*) prevail in the north except where marshes border Lake Chad, a shallow body of water which shrinks to half its size during the dry season.

Climate

Climate varies with the winds. The monsoon blowing across the Gulf of Guinea brings relatively cool air to the southwest; the northeast is hot and dusty, whipped by the *harmattan* which comes from the Sahara and cracks the lips and skin.

The seasons are well marked: two rainy seasons in the south and one in the north, where it is hot and dry for the rest of the year. Temperatures range from 71° F to 89° F (21° C to 32° C) in the south and from 66° F to 95° F (19° C to 35° C) in the north and vary little during the day.

Humidity is always high in the south, seldom below 70 percent during the daytime and as high as 95–99 percent at night. Rainfall averages 25 inches (63 cm) or less in the north. In the south, there is some rain every month of the year, averaging 80 inches (200 cm) along the coast and 150 inches (380 cm) around the Niger Delta.

Rivers

Nigeria's rivers are its outstanding geographical feature. The mighty Niger, the "Nile of the Negroes," flows 2,600 miles (4,160 km) from the mountains of Guinea to its broad delta on the gulf where it branches out like a many-fingered hand. Its fertile soils make rich farmland.

The Benue River flows west from Cameroon and forms a Y where it joins the Niger, creating a natural boundary which divides the country into three areas—north, southwest, and southeast. These areas correspond to the homelands of the three most important ethnic groups in the country: the Hausa-Fulani, the Yoruba, and the Ibo.

The Cross River is the major river of the southeast. All three rivers are important to trade. There are 5,331 miles (8,577 km) of navigable waterways.

Cities

Most Nigerians live in rural areas but 24 Nigerian cities have populations of over 100,000.

Lagos is the second largest city between Cairo and Johannesburg. (Kinshasa, the capital of Zaire, is first.) It was a Portuguese trading post and slave trade center until the British captured it in 1861. Today, it is the capital and commercial heart of Nigeria.

An aerial view of Lagos, the capital of Nigeria.

There are four island and four mainland sections in the city. Bridges between them are jammed. Traffic tie-ups snarl the streets as cars, taxis, motorbikes, and bicycles vie for space with masses of people on foot. The harbor is crowded with ships. The bustle of economic and social activity gives the city an exciting air of progress.

Lagos is a young city; 70 percent of its population is between 20 and 29 years old. But, there aren't enough jobs for everyone and the cost of food and rent are high.

The "old city" of Lagos is troubled by narrow streets, poor housing, impure water, lack of proper sanitation and electricity. The "new city," on Lagos Island, boasts luxury hotels with night-clubs and swimming pools and restaurants with Chinese, Indian, and French cooking. Most of the government buildings, offices, and shops are there, as well as the National Museum, University of Lagos, College of Technology, and a large sports stadium. People swim and fish at beautiful beaches and lagoons nearby. The residential area has tree-lined streets and palatial homes and gardens. But there are also mud-walled family compounds that have changed little in the past centuries.

Ibadan lies north of Lagos, near the old Yoruba religious center of Ife. It is still a great seat of learning. The University of Ibadan, founded in 1948, was the first in Nigeria. Ibadan is important as a trade center on the railway between the Gulf Coast and Kano.

Christians and Muslims mingle freely in Ibadan. The Blue Market is famous for handwoven Idire cloth, tie-dyed in pots of indigo; beads; thorn carvings; *juju* herbs; and Moroccan leather. Crowded and noisy like Lagos, Ibadan has over a million inhabitants and sprawls over seven hills like ancient Rome.

Kano, in Northern Nigeria, one of the seven "true Hausa

[14]

states," was the greatest commercial power in West Africa in the 1820s. Its cotton goods and red leather products were famous all over the Mediterranean. Kurmi Market was the major market between the Atlantic and the Nile. Cowrie shells were used for exchange with the Arabs who brought swordblades, weapons, salt, spices, perfumes, and printed books. Today, groundnuts (peanuts) are stacked in immense pyramids awaiting shipment south. The colonialists changed the direction of Kano's trade.

The old section of the city still exists, its flat-roofed houses surrounded by a mud wall with fourteen gates, 12¼ miles (20 km) long, 40 feet (12 m) wide, and 30 to 50 feet (9 to 15 m) high. Outside the walls stands the largest and most beautiful mosque in Nigeria. Its graceful minarets and green-tiled dome gleam in the sun.

A VARIED PEOPLE

There are over 200 different groups of people in Nigeria. Many have their own language, religion, family customs, history and traditions, and ways of governing themselves. Each is proud of its own heritage.

Some of the groups are small, with fewer than 1,000 members. But, three of them are as big as entire nations, numbering over ten million each. They are the Hausa-Fulani of the north, the Yoruba of the southwest, and the Ibo of the southeast. Together, they total over half of Nigeria's population.

Hausa-Fulani

The Hausa are the largest ethnic group in Nigeria. The traders of West Africa, they have lived in the north for 1,000 years and established great cities in olden times. They are Muslims.

[15]

Beginning in the fifteenth century, Muslim Fulani migrated into the area. In their *jihad,* or holy war, of the nineteenth century, believing the Hausa were lax in their religion, the Fulani conquered them. They intermarried with the Hausa, adopted their language, and settled in their cities where they became religious and political leaders. They form an elite aristocracy to this day. Hausa-Fulani leaders are called *emirs.*

Until the twentieth century, the Hausa had little contact with coastal peoples and they still regard outsiders with suspicion. Foreigners live in *sabon gari,* strangers' town, outside the walls of their settlements.

The Hausa social order is strict. The ruling Fulani and the Muslim religious teachers (*mallams*) are at the top. Next in importance are the traders, who are known at markets throughout West and Central Africa. Craftsmen who weave cloth and work metal are also highly regarded. Last in importance are butchers and poets!

The family is the model for Hausa society. Strict obedience is required of children and discipline is severe. Women are considered inferior and must stay within the family compound. They had little schooling in the past and have only recently gained the right to vote: in secluded polling places unseen by the eyes of others.

Fulani

No one is certain where the Fulani came from. It may have been Egypt or the Mideast. There are two groups. The "town" Fulani are settled farmers who have intermarried with the Hausa and look very like them. The country or "cow" Fulani retain the narrower nose, thinner lips, and straighter profiles of their trans-Saharan ancestors. They are very proud of their heritage and keep away from other northern groups. They are lighter in color than their town cousins who call them "red men."

The country Fulani are nomads who migrate with the seasons, seeking new pastures for their cattle as far west as Senegal and east to Cameroon. Their women, less secluded than the settled Fulani, make butter which they sell along the way. Both men and women wear their hair in long narrow braids interwoven with colored beads. Men wear short sleeveless garments draped over one shoulder like a Roman toga.

Yoruba

The Yoruba of the southwest had a mighty empire long before the Europeans reached their shores. Their kingdoms at Ife, Oyo, and Benin thrived from the twelfth to the nineteenth century.

The *oni* of Ife is the Yoruba religious leader; and the *alafin* of Oyo, their political leader. They are treated with awe and reverence and live in regal splendor.

The Yoruba are divided into many subgroups, each ruled by a chief called an *oba*. Many Yorubas are Christians, and some Muslim, but traditional native religions are still important.

The Yoruba differ from other African groups because they usually live together in large urban centers. Yoruba farmers often commute 15 or 20 miles (24 to 32 km) to their farmlands. Many of Nigeria's major cities today, including Lagos and Ibadan, are in Yorubaland.

As a people, the Yoruba have a reputation for being

While Nigeria has in recent years become a major oil-producing nation, almost three-quarters of all Nigerians still work the land or herd cattle for a living.

eager to achieve success and to acquire the modern symbols of wealth. They recognize the values of good health and education and work hard to achieve their goals. In their compounds, each man has a right to a share of the land.

Like most African groups, men have many wives, but women have rights among the Yoruba. They may even develop their own income through crafts or other industry. Women wear loose, wide-sleeved blouses and wraparound skirts in bright colors. All shades of blue are popular. Women and girls wear colorful head-ties or bandannas. Men wear long tunics over loose pants and small caps of many designs.

Ibo

The Ibo inhabit the forests and coastal regions of southeast Nigeria. They have never been unified into organized systems of government like the Hausa and Yoruba. There are many different customs and languages among them. They live in small scattered settlements, each governed by a council of elders. There are no *obas* or *emirs*.

Because they had no distinctive culture, the Ibo were most influenced by the teachings of the missionaries. They accepted European ideas enthusiastically, and became the most westernized of Nigerians.

Their knowledge of English, acquired early, gave them an advantage. So did the cultivation of palm oil, prized as a source of lubricating oil and soap, which brought them in contact with Europeans. They often migrated to work in other areas and were sometimes resented, particularly in the north where they held many government jobs.

The Ibo are ambitious to improve themselves. They call it "getting up." "Getting up" honors a person's family and village. Improved schools, pure water, better medical centers, and electrical power are some signs of achievement.

The most energetic and aggressive Nigerians, the Ibo make up 11 percent of the population of Lagos where they hold important jobs in government, trade, and the professions.

The Ibo are shorter and heavier than the Hausa and Yoruba, but they are strong and sturdy. In rural areas, they wear little except a breechcloth and skullcap; on special occasions, colorful kneelength cloth skirts, tied at the waist, and covered with a cape. Women wear blouses and a full-length sarong.

There are other important groups which number over a million people each. The Kanuri of the Chad Basin are of mixed Negro and Arab blood and like the Hausa-Fulani, are also Muslims. The Tiv are one of hundreds of less-developed groups who live in scattered areas through central Nigeria where they remain independent of their more powerful countrymen. The Edo, Ibibio, and Ijaw inhabit the southeast rain forest and the coast.

Family ties are important to all groups; a common ancestry binds people together and ancestors often play a part in religious beliefs. Men and women have different rights and roles. A man may have many wives. He pays "bridewealth" to her family for the right to marry. (Brides are getting very expensive now and are being replaced by cars as status symbols.)

Everybody wants lots of children, but children don't have many rights. In the north, parents sometimes avoid contact with a first child altogether. Older people are highly respected by everyone. Very old men are honored most; very young girls, least.

Before independence, many groups wore a particular style of dress which distinguished them from others. They decorated their faces with patterns of scars, colored their bodies and hair with red dye, and pierced their noses with straws of grain or gold rings. Today, many of the older cultural differences have disappeared, especially in the large towns and cities where European and western ways have won favor. In rural areas, however, language and customs are as varied as ever.

Language

English is the official language of Nigeria, but no single language is understood by everyone. Many Nigerians know two or more languages: their own, the language of a neighboring group, and the language most common to their area. Hausa, used throughout the north, is the most widely spoken African language.

Religion

About 45 percent of the people of Nigeria are Muslims; 35 percent are Christians. The remainder practice traditional religions based on a belief in the spirit world. Northern Nigeria is known to Muslims as the "Holy North." Christianity is strongest among the Ibo of the southeast; the southwest is a mixture. But, traditional religions flourish everywhere and all religions borrow freely from one another.

Traditional beliefs acknowledge one supreme god as Muslims and Christians do. He is *Ororun* to the Yoruba and *Chukwu* to the Ibo. Lesser gods come in contact with living people and serve as the supreme god's messengers, or as gods of prophesy, thunder and lightning, fertility, and so forth. They can cause crops to grow, rain to fall, people to prosper, children to be born, and death to occur.

There are also spirits which inhabit the natural world. Some live in trees or in animals. All natural objects have a spirit soul. It is important to please the gods for they can get very angry.

Each family or individual may have a special god that protects them, brings good fortune, or helps them achieve their goals. The spirits of family ancestors also influence one's life. Religious beliefs help unite people. People worship the gods with their dances, pipes and drums, masks, and costumes.

Islam

Islam was founded in Arabia in the seventh century by the Prophet Mohammed. Its sacred book is the Koran. It was written in Arabic. The followers of Islam are called Muslims.

A Muslim has five duties, called the Five Pillars of Islam: to affirm the faith by stating "There is no God but Allah, and Mohammed is his prophet"; to pray five times each day, facing the holy city of Mecca; to help the poor; to go without food and drink and sexual relations from dawn to dusk during the holy month of Ramadan; and, sometime in life, to make a pilgrimage (the *haj*) to far-off Mecca. Muslims must also take part in a *jihad*, or holy war, to defend the faith if their leaders call for it. In Nigeria, the *jihad* has been called twice: once against the

The Muslim teacher at left reads the Koran (the sacred book of Islam), and the children repeat his words out loud. This way, they will eventually be able to quote the Koran by heart.

Hausa states and once against the British. Islam is a way of life. Muslim laws (the *sharia*) govern its followers.

Muslims generally cover their bodies. In northern Nigeria, where Islam prevails, the men wear loose flowing robes, usually white, and wrap their heads in turbans, the end of which covers their lower face to form a veil. A white skullcap shows that the wearer is *alhaji*, a pilgrim to Mecca. Small cases containing writings in Arabic from the Koran are carried on the body to ward off disease and bring good luck. Some foods (especially pork) and all alcoholic beverages are forbidden.

A Muslim man may have four wives. Marriages are arranged by parents and often take place when girls are only fourteen. Muslim women have no legal rights. After marriage, they must wear dark garments which cover them from head to toe and live in *purdah*, secluded from the eyes of others.

AN ANCIENT HISTORY

Long before the great Sudanese empires of Ghana, Mali, and Songhai rose and fell to the west, an advanced civilization thrived in what is now central Nigeria. As early as 500 B.C., people of the Nok culture mined gold, used iron tools for farming, and molded beautiful terra-cotta sculptures.

Beginning in the ninth century, the Kanem-Bornu empire flourished under Moslem influence near Lake Chad.

Recorded history began around A.D. 1100 in the Sudan. In the centuries that followed, the Hausa established powerful city-states at Kano, Katsina, and Zaria which prospered as southern terminals of the trans-Saharan caravan routes. Berber traders from the Mediterranean and Arabs from the Red Sea brought slabs of salt, glass beads, and pottery to exchange for ivory, ebony, honey, and gold. The Berbers and Arabs also brought Islam.

In the early nineteenth century, Muslim Fulani, led by Usman dan Fodio, Commander of the Faithful, swept through Hausa territory in splendid robes and quilted armor and conquered an area of 100,000 square miles (258,998 sq km).

To the south, the Yoruba, expanding from their religious center at Ife, founded great kingdoms at Oyo and Benin. They were highly organized states with elaborate courts and well-trained armies, equipped with firearms traded by the Portuguese. The British burned Benin in 1897 in revenge for the deaths of a party of traders. They sacked the palace and carried off royal treasure, including works of art in ivory, wood, bronze, and brass, which astounded the European world.

Coming of the Europeans

The adventurous Portuguese were the first Europeans to enter the Gulf of Guinea. They set up their first trading stations along the coast, near Benin, in 1486. By the eighteenth century, the British and French had replaced them as the chief traders of the Slave Coast.

The slave trade brought to a standstill the social and economic progress which earlier civilizations had made.

After the British outlawed slavery in 1807, they found Nigeria a rich source of raw materials and a promising market for their manufactured goods. Africans who had prospered from the slave trade opposed its ending. With their efforts to end the trade and to develop their commercial interests, British domination increased. Rivalries among coastal groups, and their eagerness to share the benefits of European trade, led them to cooperate and to accept British political, religious, and economic control.

Trade continued mostly with the coastal regions. The interior with its intense heat, high humidity, and diseases like malaria, sleeping sickness, and yellow fever, was known as the "white man's graveyard." The discovery of quinine as a cure for malaria helped after 1880.

Explorers

A fearless Scottish doctor, Mungo Park, began to explore the interior in 1795. He lost his life while seeking the mouth of the Niger River when he drowned fleeing attackers. The Lander brothers, Richard and John, who were English, reached the Delta in 1830. Richard was wounded and died on a later expedition.

The Royal Niger Company, a trading company originally founded in 1879 by Sir George Goldie, a Niger River trader, helped to open the north, subdue the Fulani, and drive off the French and Germans to assure British claims.

In 1885, British claims to a "sphere of influence" in Nigeria were recognized by the European powers meeting in Berlin. British explorers and missionaries and traders and, when necessary, the force of arms helped to secure the colony for the crown.

Missionaries

Hand in hand with the traders and explorers came the missionaries. In their attempt to exchange the "benefits of European civilization" for traditional customs and beliefs which they considered "savage," the missionaries sometimes did more harm than good. But, their establishment of schools and hospitals helped. Many of modern Nigeria's leaders have come from the small groups they educated.

Colonialism

In 1914, the northern and southern areas and Lagos were united as the British Colony and Protectorate of Nigeria.

Under the British, traditional rivalry between the north and south grew. In order to rule more easily in the north, the British governed through the ruling Fulani emirs. Few taxes were collected, roads were poor, and farming methods were primitive. Because there were no missionaries among the Muslims, schools and medical services were also inferior.

In the south, meanwhile, profitable trade brought income from customs duties. Roads and railroads were built, harbors dredged, and cities modernized. English was taught in the schools and Africans held positions in the colonial administration.

Nigerian Nationalism

Protests against colonial rule began as early as 1895 with an attack on the Royal Niger Company. There were tax revolts and war protests and the expression of local grievances. At the end of the nineteenth century, many church groups broke away from their European parent bodies and became a force for independence and improved social conditions.

As early as 1922, Africans were given some voice in the government. Following World War II, the British helped draft constitutions that moved Nigeria toward self-government.

On October 1, 1960, Nigeria became the sixteenth African state to achieve independence as a federation of the three geographical regions and Lagos, under a parliamentary form of government. Three years later, it became a republic within the British Commonwealth of Nations. Abubakar Tafawa Balewa became prime minister. He was a Muslim from the north, but he spoke for national unity and progress. Nnamdi Azikiwe, known as "Zik," was the first president. A Protestant from Iboland, he studied in the United States and led the movement for national independence.

In spite of economic gains after independence, ethnic and regional rivalries continued, corruption existed, and riots led to a breakdown in order. In 1966, an Ibo group overthrew and assassinated Balewa and proclaimed military rule. Six months later, there were further killings. Lieutenant Colonel Yakubu "Jack" Gowon, a young military officer from the north, took power. When several thousand Ibos who held government positions in the north were killed in battles with the Hausa, hundreds of thousands headed home to southeast Nigeria. Attempts to calm unrest failed, and on May 30, 1967, the Ibos withdrew from Nigeria and declared independence as the Republic of Biafra. All schools closed, and economic progress stopped for thirty months until Biafra surrendered on January 15, 1970. Over a million Biafrans died, many of starvation, in spite of world efforts to help. General Gowon won praise for helping the Ibos regain their place in Nigerian life where they play an important role today.

A third military coup, in 1975, overthrew Gowon who went into exile in England. The new leader, Brigadier General Murtala Ramat Mohammed, was also an army man and a Fulani. He was a popular leader, but when a census showed there were many more northerners than had been supposed, fear and resentment grew in the south, and Mohammed was assassinated in 1976. Olusegun Obasanjo replaced him and served until military rule ended in the fall of 1979. Alhaji Shehu Shagari, a 55-year-old poet, teacher, and businessman, was elected president. The new government is structured much like ours, with a president, vice president, senate, house of representatives, and a federal system of nineteen states.

A GROWING NATION

Nigeria was once, like most African countries, dependent on agriculture for its national wealth. Most Nigerians were farmers who worked on small farms to raise a few crops for food and a few more for sale. Then, enormous supplies of oil were discovered in the Delta. Oil production began in 1958. In twenty years, Nigeria has become the sixth largest oil producer in the world, producing over two million barrels a day!

The civil war slowed development, and traffic jams and port congestion added problems, but in some years, oil accounts for as much as 95 percent of all exports. The United States is the biggest customer. We import $10 billion of Nigeria's oil a year. With exports to Nigeria of machinery, transport equipment, and manufactured goods, we rank third behind Britain and West Germany.

Nigeria has other mineral resources, too—tin, coal, columbite, and natural gas among them. In 1969, a $245 million dam and hydroelectric plant opened. It could produce a million kilowatts of power for the growing economy.

Oil revenues have helped finance cement plants; a natural gas project; lumber, plywood, and textile mills; and agricultural development. After the war, roads and railways were improved, radio, television, and telephone service expanded, and a modern airline system developed. More engineers and technicians are being trained.

About 70 percent of the people still work in agriculture. Cocoa, palm products, groundnuts, and rubber are important exports. "Operation Feed the Nation" began in 1976. Its goal is to produce enough food for everyone. Food production had gone down as production of cash crops went up. Oil income was used to finance public works and construction projects. A five-year development plan for 1975–80 called for spending $50 billion to improve Nigeria's standard of living. The government hopes to lessen its dependency on oil by boosting agriculture with better seeds and fertilizer and modern equipment.

Health

If you were born in Nigeria, you could expect to live about 41 years. Life expectancy in the United States is 73.

A Methodist missionary society built the first hospital in Nigeria, in 1912. For many years, missionaries were alone in fighting disease. Today, organizations like WHO (World Health Organization) and UNICEF (United Nations International Children's Emergency Fund) and United States AID (Agency for International Development) help combat the threats to life and health which plague Nigeria and other sub-Saharan nations: poor food and not enough of it, polluted water, lack of proper sanitation (open sewers are common), inadequate medical facilities and supplies.

Traditionally, men have first call on the available food. Women and children get what's left. (Children are sometimes discouraged from eating meat or eggs because they may not be able to afford them when they grow up.) As a result, many children suffer from malnutrition. Foods are mostly grains (millet, maize, and rice) or root crops (sorghum, yams, cassava), starchy foods which are ground into gruel or mush. They lack important vitamins and animal protein. This retards growth and reduces energy and resistance to disease.

Pneumonia and malaria are the chief causes of death in Nigeria. Vaccination has eliminated smallpox and helped reduce measles as a cause of infant death, but half of all children die before they reach the age of five. Mothers carry their babies to market on their backs, exposing them to infectious diseases. Insect control attempts to contain malaria. Sleeping sickness, carried by the tsetse fly, is a major problem. There are 50,000 lepers in Nigeria. Missions help care for the most serious cases.

Traditional ways of curing, by witch doctors and medicine men, are still popular. Because Africans have long suffered from disease, the early death of their children, and other misfortunes, they needed to find causes and cures they could believe in. There are all kinds of herbs, salves, and incenses made of leaves, roots, and barks. Dried kaga nut soaked in water is applied to snake bites; strings of beads or dolls are carried as charms to protect the bearer from disease; dried owl feet, elephant skin, snake heads, lion tails, and antelope horn are common treatments. A witch doctor, or *juju* man, sprinkles cassava flour on a newlywed couple to bring them healthy children. Some remedies help, but some—like bush tea—are fatal.

The government has expanded medical schools and some doctors have come from other countries. Health insurance and maternity benefits, as well as workmen's compensation and social security, are provided. Still, there is only one hospital bed for every 2,900 people and one doctor for every 24,000.

Education

More than anything else, young Nigerians today want a good education. They realize that education will help them get jobs and will teach them better ways to raise crops for food and market. Education prepares them for positions in government, trade, or industry; and makes it possible for them to help other Nigerians improve their life.

Only one of every four people in Nigeria knows how to read and write. In the north of the country, the figures are even lower. The government is trying to increase literacy but it is costly.

Christian mission schools brought western education to southern Nigeria, beginning in 1842. Boys attended Muslim schools in the north to study Arabic script and the Koran. Until World War II, church schools started by Europeans educated 97 percent of the students.

Today, primary schools are free for everyone. Three million students attend 16,000 schools. This is only 30 percent of the children, however, and two-thirds of them leave school before receiving their certificate. In Lagos, 88 percent finish the primary grades, but only 27 percent in the northern areas of the country. There are 212 students for every teacher.

Boys and girls speak in local dialects in school until third grade when everyone uses English. They study geography, history, arithmetic, handwriting, nature, religion, hygiene, physical education, cooking, needlework, handicrafts, and drawing.

Students must pass an examination to go on to secondary school. Most of these are boarding schools and each school has its own uniform and school colors which the students wear with pride. Few people can afford these schools, however, and many families make great sacrifices to enable their children to attend.

The University of Ibadan was founded in 1948, and today there are a dozen colleges in Nigeria and a higher proportion of university graduates than in any other sub-Saharan country. Many young people study abroad as well.

Literacy is growing. There are two dozen newspapers in Nigeria as well as radio and television. Ahmadu Bello University in the north is the largest in sub-Saharan Africa, and the Institute of African Studies at the University of Ibadan attracts scholars from all over the world.

Nigeria's new civilian government hopes to provide food and shelter and better health and education for all its people.

A RICH CULTURE

The ancient Nigerians were great sculptors. The terra-cotta heads of Nok and the bronzes of Benin are famous. The Benin sculptors worked with the "lost wax" method known to the Nile Valley and still in use today: they made a clay model, covered it with wax, and, when the wax hardened, added another layer of clay. A hot furnace melted the wax, then they poured melted bronze into the mold. The bronze filled the space where the wax had been. When the outer cover of clay was removed, the bronze was polished until it gleamed like gold. Their sculpture was used in religious ceremonies and honored their kings with scenes of warriors preparing for battle, portrait heads, and lifelike animals.

Wood carvings, between 200 and 300 years old, came from the Cross River area. Nigerians today make beautiful objects, too: carved figures in wood; decorated gourds called *calabashes*; leather, metal, and beaded works; and handwoven textiles. They also decorate their houses with colorful designs.

Although there was no written literature before the twentieth century, there are fine writers in Nigeria today. The novels of Cyprian Ekwensi, Amos Tutuola, and Chinua Achebe are read in our country, too. Wole Soyinka is a noted playwright.

Africans learn to sing and dance as soon as they learn to walk and talk. Dance has been called the "soul of Africa." Nigerian dances are often religious ceremonies which celebrate important events like birth, death, and marriage or hope to influence the gods to bring rain or plentiful crops or a good hunt. The dancers wear carved masks. Flutes and horns play. And, always, there are the drums. Some are called "talking drums" because they are pitched like speech. African people often make up their songs and dances as they go along. Popular music called Juju, Highlife, or Afrobeat combines traditional African rhythms with western styles . . . which, after all, came to us from Africa, in the first place!

For Nigerian youngsters,
dance is a natural way to
celebrate any important event.

3

CAMEROON

Cameroon is a crossroads. It is wedged between West and Central Africa at the hinge of the continent where the bulge ends and the coastline turns south, halfway between Senegal and South Africa.

In colonial times, Cameroon felt the domination of Germany, France, and Britain, and today it is the only country in Africa with two official languages: French and English.

There are over 200 different ethnic groups in Cameroon. In many cases, people feel more loyal to their own customs and traditions than to the new national government. This has slowed progress toward unification in Cameroon, as it has in many sub-Saharan nations.

Colonial rule, however, tried to keep peace among rival groups and, since then, modern communications and the move to the cities have helped bring people closer. The change from small-scale farming, which provided a family's food, to growing cash crops on large plantations, where many groups work together, has tended to break down differences, too.

At independence in 1960, Cameroon shared with many other sub-Saharan nations a low level of economic development. A stable government, under the same leadership for twenty years, has allowed it to make slow but steady advances toward improving the lives of its people.

THE LAND

Cameroon is shaped like a triangle. Its base is at the inner curve or "hinge" of the West African hump, and its peak nears the southern edge of the Sahara, thrusting into the waters of Lake Chad. Its area, 183,398 square miles (475,442 sq km), is a little larger than California.

It is bounded by Nigeria on the northwest; Chad and the Central African Republic on the east; Congo, Gabon, and Equatorial Guinea on the south; and 250 miles (400 km) of coastline along the Gulf of Guinea.

There is every variety of sub-Saharan land and plantlife within its borders. From the flood marshes of the Chad Basin, semiarid savannas with sparse tough grasses and scrubby thornbush broaden into grasslands dotted with scattered acacia trees, then climb steeply to a rugged wooded plateau, with elevations between 2,500 and 4,500 feet (750 and 1,350 km).

Forested mountain ranges stretch along the western border, from the Mandaras in the north to the spectacular volcanic hills of the south, capped by Mt. Cameroon, 13,353 feet (4,070 m), the highest peak in sub-Saharan West Africa.

A coastal plain from 10 to 50 miles (16 to 80 km) wide curves along the Gulf of Guinea in the southwest. It is thick with sluggish lagoons and mangrove swamps and dotted with a few beautiful beaches. Beyond it, a dense rain forest stretches for 300 miles (485 km) into the interior.

A tangle of trees, plants, and vines, dank and dark, dense and forbidding, marks the rain forest. Ebony, mahogany, and other hardwoods and many varieties of ferns and exotic orchids grow vigorously in this moist environment. Evergreen trees, choked with clinging vines and mosses, grow thick and close together, reaching heights of 200 feet (60 m). Their topmost branches, seeking the sun, tower over the leafy canopy which keeps the ground below in almost continuous shadow. Humidity is seldom below 50 percent in the rain forest and often about 80 percent.

Cameroon has many rivers. The Benue, which flows northwestward into Nigeria to join the Niger, nourishes vegetation along its banks and forms a boundary between northern and central Cameroon. Splendid waterfalls mark the course of the Sanaga, which separates the central and southern regions. Only the waters of the Benue are suitable for navigation. At their peak, from July to September, they carry barge traffic to and from Nigeria. Garoua is an important inland port.

Douala, the most important seaport in Cameroon and its center of commerce, is located near the mouth of the Wouri River. Mt. Cameroon looms above it. There are large new buildings there and some fine hotels and restaurants and outdoor cafes overlooking public squares. A modern water system has been installed and roads, railways, and an international airport

*Cameroon has a wide variety of land and plant life, from
the beaches along the Gulf of Guinea, to the top of Mt.
Cameroon, to the semiarid land in the south, pictured here.*

connect it with other important cities. It is a melting pot for Cameroon's people and bustles with activity, but unemployment and the rising cost of living are continuing problems.

Climate

Cameroon lies entirely within the Torrid Zone or Tropics. Its temperature range is slight, averaging between 70–82° F (21–28° C) year round.

A hot, dry, semidesert climate prevails in the north, where annual rainfall averages less than 30 inches (75 cm). A long dry season, from October to April, brings dry winds from the Sahara and the fierce dust storms of the *harmattan,* which cause herdsmen to seek cover for their animals and shelter for themselves. Crops such as cotton and groundnuts can be grown in the north under favorable conditions.

The central plateaus average twice as much rain as the north. A pleasant climate, like that of the U.S. western prairies, prevails at the higher elevations, with periods of low humidity and moderate temperatures.

Descending southward from the plateaus, moving from wooded savannah and open grasslands into equatorial rain forest, the weather becomes muggy and humid.

The climate along the coast has been compared to a Turkish bath. Clouds, heavy rain, and high humidity constantly surround the area. Two wet seasons, in the spring and late summer, shower 152.5 inches (386 cm) of rain on south Cameroon yearly. Winds from the Gulf of Guinea bring downpours which make the coastal area one of the wettest spots on earth. The western slopes of Mt. Cameroon have recorded 360 inches (900 cm) of rain in one year! Yet, this is an area of great fertility with rich volcanic soils where the cultivation of bananas, cocoa, coffee, rubber, and timber thrives.

Wildlife

Monkeys screech, parrots squawk, and pythons slither through the dank green rain forest. Small flying mice glide from tree to tree in the mountains of the west. Big game fish, tarpon and barracuda, stalk the coastal waters. Quarrelsome baboons are almost everywhere and a few surviving elephants roam at large in the forest woodlands.

Cameroon protects its wildlife, controls hunting, and has set aside 1.6 million acres (640,000 hectares) of preserves. There are six large national parks north of Ngaoundere. Waza National Park, established in 1934, is one of the best in West Africa.

It is possible to see elephant, giraffe, rhino, hippo, buffalo, crocodile, many varieties of antelope, lion, leopard, and chee-tah. Gorillas and chimps and colorful birds inhabit the forests. The rivers are rich with fish—catfish, carp, perch, and tilapia—and the swamps and lagoons with birds—flamingoes, ibis, king-fishers, storks, ostriches, guinea hens, geese, cranes, ospreys, and pelicans.

There are all varieties of creeping things—frogs that grow as large as dogs, lizards, toads, small vipers, rodents and bats, and all kinds of bugs and insects. The dreaded tsetse fly, which spreads sleeping sickness, plagues Cameroon, as it does many other African countries, and mosquitoes carry yellow fever and malaria.

*Rhinoceroses are only some of the unusual
—and large—animals to be found in Cameroon.*

THE PEOPLE

Cameroon has been called the *racial crossroads* of Africa because so many different ethnic groups have come from other parts of the continent to settle and intermingle there. There are as many as 200 ethnic groups with many different languages, customs, and social systems among the 8 million people in Cameroon today.

Berbers came from the Mediterranean coast north of the Sahara. Arabs, from the east, reached Cameroon in the eighteenth century. Fulani tribes from the west were there as early as the 1300s. In the eighteenth and nineteenth centuries, fighting their holy war for Islam, the Fulani conquered many of the earlier settlers and made them their slaves.

The descendants of the Fulani, who live in the north of Cameroon today, account for only a third of the people there, but their influence is far greater than their numbers. They are a ruling class who hire others to work for them. People have been known to barter their children to the Fulani in exchange for food.

The Fulani are very proud of their Muslim heritage and refer to those who follow the traditional religions as *kirdi* or pagans. To escape Fulani domination, many non-Muslims have fled to the hills and settled in small villages where they support themselves by growing millet and other foods.

Central Cameroon was the original home of the Bantu before they began migrating to the east and south of Africa. The Bamileke, a semi-Bantu group, account for about 30 percent of the population. There are about 2 million of them. Called "grasslanders," they inhabit the western and central highlands. They live in huts of mud and straw. Cone-shaped roofs, like Indian tepees, allow the rain to flow off. Bamboo fences help keep out wild animals and unwanted visitors. Increasing numbers of Bamileke are settling in the cities now, where they hold 70 percent of the professional jobs and 30 percent of the government positions. The Fulani, who are their traditional enemies, resent this.

The south is the home of the Guinea Coast or "true" Negro. Some have crossed the border from southern Nigeria, seeking jobs in Cameroon. They include the Ibo, Ibidio, Ijaw, Ekoi, and Edo. There are about 20,000 Europeans and Americans in Cameroon.

In the denseness of the southern rain forest, small bands of Pygmies still forage and hunt as they have for centuries. Pygmy is a Greek word of measurement, the distance between the elbow and the knuckles, and Pygmies average between 4 feet 3 inches and 4 feet 9 inches (147 to 162 cm) in height. Their small size helps them move easily through the forest; their yellow-brown skin helps camouflage them; and their short sturdy legs are good for climbing trees.

Pygmies travel through the forest in search of wild game— antelope, monkeys, birds, elephants, and buffalo—which they shoot with spears or bows with poison-tipped arrows. They also set traps, fish with nets, and gather nuts and honey and medicinal plants. They venture out of the forest only to trade with the settled villagers beyond its borders, exchanging their goods for salt, metal spearheads, groundnuts, and other foods. Sometimes they are asked to take part in village ceremonies, in hopes they will keep the forest spirits from doing harm to the villagers.

Pygmies live in small huts made of the leafy branches of palm or banana trees, which they can put up in a few hours.

When they move to a new hunting ground, they abandon them. Unlike most Africans, Pygmies have only one wife. They have no political organization, but each age group has its own responsibilities. They call themselves *bamiki ba'ndura*—children of the forest.

The population of Cameroon averages about 46 people per square mile (17 per sq km). Some parts of the country, especially the north, are more sparsely settled. Scattered areas of the Mandara Mountains in the northwest, between Garoua and Maroua, are heavily populated by the non-Muslim hill people who congregate in villages and towns and support themselves with farming and herding. The major areas of population concentration are the seaport of Douala and Yaounde, the capital, where population averages 100 to 300 a square mile (30 to 90 a sq km). About 20 percent of the people live in the cities.

Language
Cameroon's colonial history has given the country two official languages, French and English. But there are 24 other major languages and many local dialects, including Wes Cos, a slang which developed among blacks during the days of the slave trade and still serves as a form of communication between peoples of the north and south.

Religion
About half the people of Cameroon follow traditional religions based on a belief in a spirit world. About 30 percent of the people are Christians, more Roman Catholic than Protestant. The remaining people, mostly in the north, are Muslim.

[45]

Health

People who live near the cities in the south have better health care than those in the "bush," as the country is called in Africa. There is only one hospital bed for every 323 people and one doctor for 27,000. Many infants die in the first year of their lives. Poor diet causes malnutrition. Poor sanitation spreads disease. Malaria and tuberculosis are the worst problems. But there is also *kwashiorkor,* caused by lack of animal protein; bilharziasis (snail fever), which is common in streams and ponds around Lake Chad; and *onchocerciasis* (river blindness), which is spread by mosquitoes and flies which breed in open sewers. Rivers, pools, and other bodies of water often serve for washing clothes and food as well as drinking water for animals and humans. They are often polluted by both. Few people have running water. Girls may walk several miles to collect a days' supply of water, which they carry home in jugs balanced on their heads.

Folk medicines are popular. Since many ailments are believed to be the work of evil spirits, magic acts and sacrifice are sometimes called upon to cure them. Herbal medicines are widely used.

The United States helps Cameroon with a Food for Peace program and helps fund the University Center for Health Sciences.

The bustling city of Douala, Cameroon's most important seaport.

Education

Most of Cameroon's children (65–70 percent) go to grade school. As a result, a high number of Cameroon's adult population knows how to read and write. Although there is a shortage of teachers, Cameroon's school system is extensive. It has tried to ensure equal education for all parts of the country. It is hoped this will help to unify the nation and aid its development. The University of Yaounde teaches courses in both English and French. Peace Corps volunteers from the United States help teach English.

HISTORY

The name Cameroon comes from the Portuguese. Portuguese explorers, in 1472, sailed into the Bight of Biafra and named the Wouri River *Rio dos Camaroes,* for a kind of shellfish which they caught in its coastal waters.

But sailors from ancient Carthage, on the north shore of Africa, visited the country as early as 500 B.C. and discovered the majestic peaks of Mt. Cameroon which they named "Chariot of the Gods."

From the eleventh to the eighteenth century, the northern part of the country was fought over by a number of great African empires, including Kanem-Bornu. People came from across the Sahara to settle in the Sudan. The Fulani gained control of the north and established the Muslim religion there. Bantus made their home in the central regions, Pygmies in the southern forests, and Guinea Coast Negroes in the southern coastal areas.

All of Cameroon, like all of Africa south of the Sahara, was black. At first, few Europeans ventured beyond the coast.

Tangled mangrove swamps, dense forests, and swarms of disease-bearing insects kept them from moving inland. But, as early as the sixteenth century, lured by gold, ivory, and spices, trade with the interior began. Later, in the seventeenth and eighteenth centuries, the infamous slave trade expanded it.

Colonial Cameroon
The Portuguese were followed by the Dutch, who set up the first trading post on the mainland, in the 1640s. Spanish, Scandinavians, and French also visited the area. The British, who had outlawed slavery in their own dominions in 1807, made the first permanent settlement in Cameroon, at Victoria. It was a church mission. Missionaries helped rout out and abolish the slave trade. Palm oil and ivory became the major items of commerce. Trade with the Europeans helped strengthen the African tribes (including the Bassa, Bamileke, and Douala) who served as middlemen with the interior. They often received firearms in return for their goods.

In 1884, before the British and French had a chance to consolidate their influence in Cameroon, Germany signed treaties with the Douala chieftains which enabled it to declare a "protectorate" over the area, which it called *Kamerun*.

After Germany's defeat in World War I, Cameroon was split between the British and the French and ruled as a League of Nations mandate. Four-fifths of Kamerun, in the east, became *Cameroun*, a part of French Equatorial Africa; one-fifth, in the west, became *the Cameroons*, a part of the British Empire. Black Africans made little progress under this system and, under the French, sometimes endured forced labor in addition to denial of political rights.

Following World War II, in which Cameroon became a Free French territory, British and French rule continued. Both areas were administered as United Nations trusteeships, the British territory as part of Nigeria. Conditions improved and the people were given an increasing role in their own government.

Independence

Cameroon was caught up in the nationalist fervor which swept the continent in the '50s. But differences between ethnic groups and political factions kept the country in turmoil for a decade.

Ahmadou Ahidjo, a moderate, emerged as the leader of a strife-torn nation. He was a northerner and the son of a Fulani chief. In February 1958, he became prime minister and, with the help of French troops, eventually quelled unrest.

On January 1, 1960, French Cameroon became an independent republic.

Unification

In 1961, the northern part of British Cameroon voted to become part of Nigeria; the southern part, to join with the former French territory as the Federal Republic of Cameroon.

In 1972, another referendum created the United Republic of Cameroon, a single unitary state with one national assembly.

Ahidjo has been president since independence and was elected to a fifth five-year term in 1980. In his efforts to achieve national unity and economic development, he has ruled with strong executive authority and maintained strict control of press, radio, student activity, and political association. There is a single political party.

ECONOMY

Under a strong and stable government for twenty years, Cameroon has done better than most newly independent sub-Saharan nations.

Almost 80 percent of the people are farmers. The country's major exports are agricultural products: coffee, cocoa, and timber. Bananas, rubber, cotton, groundnuts, and palm oil are also important. Cocoa is still grown mostly on small family farms, but other crops are cultivated on big plantations. Farming methods are being modernized. Having a lot of products helps. If one has a poor growing season, or prices drop, or demand slows down, the others can make up the loss.

Cameroon's industry is growing steadily, helping it become less dependent on farm crops. About 200 small plants produce consumer goods. There is a large aluminum factory. Some oil has been found. It and a gas industry have strong potential as sources of future wealth.

Transportation has been a problem. Seasonal floods block many roadways. The completion of the Trans-Cameroonian railway between Douala and Ngaoundere and the renovation of the link between Douala and Yaounde have given a boost to the economy. The port of Douala has been expanded and the road system between Cameroon and its neighbors improved. And, like Nigeria, Cameroon has a good air transport system.

The government encourages foreign businessmen to invest in Cameroon and many have, although France still plays a major role in its economy.

Cameroon treads a middle road in world affairs. Friendly with both Western and communist countries, it remains "nonaligned," identifying with other Third World nations rather than the big world powers.

ART

When Afo-A-Kom, a carved wooden figure believed by the Kom of Cameroon to be the soul of their people, was stolen in 1966, the people went into mourning. Upon its safe return seven years later, there was a great celebration with singing, dancing, feasting, and many pots of palm wine.

Art has always been a part of life in Cameroon. Art gives prestige to its kings and chieftains, and decorates their palaces and furniture. Trumpets carved of elephant tusk or cast in metal herald their approach. Masks, often in animal form, give strength and power to the wearer and inspire fear and awe in the observer. They protect against the evil forces of the spirit world. Music and dance are part of all religious ceremonies.

Men carry wooden stools to meetings. The king's stool is ornate. No one else can sit on it. It serves as a sort of throne. Sometimes it is carved with figures of captured enemies or the royal leopard. A carved elephant tusk may serve as a footrest.

Ordinary people have made art a part of their lives, too. Tobacco pipes of clay, wood, or metal; drinking vessels of cow horn or gourd (the king's are buffalo horn); and ivory anklets and bracelets are used by all. Beadwork is a symbol of wealth, and decoration with cowrie shells, once a form of exchange, is common.

CENTRAL AFRICAN REPUBLIC (CAR)

Untouched by the great African empires of the past and unknown to much of the modern world, the Central African Republic is one of the poorest nations in the world today. With an annual income of less than $200 per person (one-third that of Nigeria, and one half that of Cameroon), it is one of the least developed countries in sub-Saharan Africa.

People of the CAR have an average life expectancy of 41 years. They are victims of poor food, unsafe water, lack of education, inadequate health care and sanitation facilities, dirt, and disease.

They have a fragile economy based on farming for food and a few cash crops, which offers them little protection against a poor growing season or a decline in demand for their products.

Isolated, underdeveloped, sparsely populated, and in the dreaded tsetse fly zone, the country also suffered in recent years from the unpredictable behavior of Emperor Bokassa I who dreamed of being another Napoleon.

Yet, the future is not without hope.

[53]

This poor country is rich in diamonds which were a major source of income in the early 70s. Production has fallen off since, but significant deposits of uranium exist, as well as some copper, iron, and tin.

Timber is plentiful. Agricultural land is well watered and fertile. Fine nature preserves and spectacular scenery and waterfalls are attractions for tourists.

Under a new government, the CAR continues its struggle to realize the potential of these resources and to create a better life for its people.

THE LAND

The CAR is a landlocked country, almost as big as Texas, located in the very heart of Africa. It is bordered by Cameroon, Chad, Sudan, Zaire, and Congo.

Most of its area is rolling plateau, covered with open savanna and dry forest. The northeast is semidesert, hot and dry, with an average rainfall of 31.5 inches (80 cm). Dense rain forest, extending eastward from Nigeria and Cameroon, covers the southwest. There are minor mountain ranges in the northeast and southeast.

Central Africa's temperature is generally warm and sunny. There is a dry season from December to April. Average annual temperature at Bangui, the capital, ranges from 72° F to 92° F (22° C to 33° C). In January and February, the dusty winds of the *harmattan* cool the north. It is quite cool in the western highlands, too.

A long rainy season, from May to November, brings about 70 inches (180 cm) of rain to the south annually. Rains are lighter and the rainy season shorter in the north.

[54]

Two major river systems water the country. The Ubangi River is suitable for navigation during most of the year and trade flows south along its waters to join the Zaire (Congo) River at the border of Congo and Zaire and flow on to the sea, over 1,100 miles (1,770 km) away, at Pointe Noire in the Congo Republic. The Shari River flows north to Lake Chad.

The country is sparsely populated, with fewer than 10 people per square mile (3 per sq km). Big game still roams at large in the mostly uninhabited eastern areas.

Cities

Bangui, the capital, founded by the French in 1891, is a pleasant town on the Ubangi River near the Zaire border. It is named for the rapids formed by the river as it flows through a nearby range of hills. There are beautiful falls 55 miles (90 km) north at Boali.

The town is crowded, especially at market time, when it is full of activity, but the streets are broad and shaded by mango trees and flowering shrubs.

Bangui is CAR's major port and most of the country's international trade passes through it. Luxury river boats dock along its banks. There is some light industry, including textiles, processed foods, shoes, and soap.

The best roads in the country radiate from Bangui, including the only route from west to east across the continent.

WILDLIFE

In his book, *My African Journey,* Winston Churchill wrote about "Birds . . . as bright as butterflies; butterflies . . . as big as birds. . . ." He might have had Central Africa in mind, for it is rich in exotic birdlife and thousands of rare and beautiful butterflies make its rain forest a collector's paradise. There are butterflies with metallic-blue wings; others are brilliant red and pale violet. Some are all colors of the rainbow.

CAR is the best place outside East Africa to see wild game. Although ivory hunters at one time shrunk the elephant herds, and annual hunting expeditions by villagers who burn vast areas of forest and grassland have cut down others, many animals have survived because nearly two-thirds of the country is uninhabited. There are about 30,000 elephant roaming the CAR today. It has been called their last great refuge.

Seven wildlife preserves and three national parks make the country a huge natural zoo, the home of buffalo and antelope (waterbuck, hartebeeste, roan, Buffon's kob, Derby eland, and great kudu) as well as the big cats (lion, leopard, and cheetah), and elephant, giraffe, hippo, and rhino.

THE PEOPLE

There are eight major ethnic groups in the Central African Republic with as many as 80 subgroups, each with its own language. About 300,000 Banda inhabit the central highlands, and an equal number of Baya live in the southwest. Both are Bantu-speaking peoples whose society is based on family ties, with the father as headman and all descendants of common ancestors members of the same group. The M'Baka, although only 7 percent of the population, are prominent and served as middlemen for the colonial administrators. They live in the most populous area of the country, along the Ubangi River where they fish and trade in dugout canoes. Ubangi women were famous in the past for stretching their lips with 6 to 8-inch (15–

20-cm) platters of wood or ivory. Boganda and Bokassa were landed members of the M'Baka; so is David Dacko.

Other groups include the Sara in the north, near Chad, and the Mandjia, who intermingle with the Baya in the southwest. About 10,000 Pygmies live in the rain forest and Fulani cattleherders and nomadic Chad Arabs and Sudanese move in and out across the borders with the seasons. Some Nilotes live in the east. They are taller and thinner than the others.

There are a few political refugees from Sudan and Zaire and about 9,000 Europeans who live mostly in Bangui.

More than 70 percent of the population lives in small villages among the coffee and cotton fields and rolling green hills. They are very like the *kibbutzim,* or communes, of Israel. Women cultivate the fields and grow food crops (sorghum, groundnuts, and bananas) around their huts. They take the cotton to market in huge rope baskets carried on their heads. Men are in charge of hunting and fishing—and fighting, if necessary. It is dishonorable for them to till the fields beyond the age of fifteen.

There are many fishing communities along the rivers.

People in the "bush," or country areas, perform lively dances in village ceremonies. Drums and horns accompany them. Basketwork is simple and practical, for use in field or household. Woodcarving is especially fine near the Congo border. There is some ivory carving, too.

French is the official language of the CAR, but very few people know how to speak it. Sangho, the language of a Ubangi River group, is a *lingua franca,* understood by nearly all groups and widely used in government. Swahili is spoken in the east, Arabic in the north, and Hausa by traders.

Over half the people practice traditional, or *animist*, religions based on a belief in a spirit world. About 40 percent are Christians, mostly Roman Catholic. There are some Muslims (about 8 percent) in the north.

Education

All poor countries suffer from a lack of education. CAR is no exception. A mere 18 percent of its people can read and write. Most of the children who go to school attend the primary grades only, where there is one teacher for every 70 students. Only one in ten go on to the 25 high schools or the few technical schools and teacher-training institutes and agricultural college. Jean-Bédel Bokassa University, offering courses in law, science, and medicine, was established in Bangui in 1974. About 300 students attend. Some young Central Africans attend college abroad, mostly in France.

Health

Disease is widespread in the CAR. Tuberculosis causes many deaths. Mosquitoes carry malaria; the tsetse fly spreads sleeping sickness; and parasites in the water cause *bilharziasis,* causing loss of blood and damage to body tissues. There are few hospitals and medical facilities: one hospital bed for every 500

Girls draw water from an unprotected community well in Yimbi, Central African Republic. Note the houses in the background with tin and thatched roofs.

[59]

people and one doctor for every 28,000. Proper sanitation and effective insect control are badly needed. Poor diet, causing malnutrition, is a major problem. Little has been done to improve conditions. Bokassa spent most of his country's funds for personal use. The United Nations and other international organizations help to educate the people and to provide immunization and the French have contributed money for health, education, and food.

HISTORY

People probably lived in the CAR before 1000 B.C., but we know little of their early history. Huge stone monuments weighing three to four tons, found along the banks of streams near Bouar, tell of an ancient culture. But no written records exist.

Slave raids of the eighteenth century wiped out much of the early population. There was a large influx of settlers during the nineteenth century when people (including the Baya and Banda) sought haven from Arab slave traders on the Nile and Europeans on the Atlantic. They found a safe home in the uninhabited interior which slave traders had difficulty in penetrating.

Colonial Rule

French military expeditions moved into Central Africa beginning in 1887 and soon crushed the resistance of its African people. The territory was part of French Equatorial Africa and became a popular big-game hunting ground for the colonialists. French companies exploited the country and practiced forced labor. Rebellions were severely repressed.

France did little to prepare its territories for independence. Less than 1 percent of its budget went to education. Poor schools, inadequate health care, and wide unemployment were common. Control was often in the hands of charter companies and their armies, or administrators who lived in France and were unfamiliar with local problems.

After World War II, during which the country served as an important base for the Free French under Charles de Gaulle, the colony was granted its own assembly, French citizenship, and representation in the French parliament. Political parties were formed.

Barthélémy Boganda, a former Catholic priest and a promising political leader, was recognized as a strong voice for African nationalism. He was the country's first prime minister.

Independence

When Boganda was killed in an air crash, his nephew David Dacko, a mild-mannered thirty-year-old school teacher and union leader, succeeded him. CAR became independent on August 13, 1960, with Dacko as president.

In spite of French loans and technical assistance, the country did not prosper. In January 1966, Col. Jean-Bédel Bokassa (Boganda's nephew) overthrew Dacko, his cousin, in a military coup, dissolved the national assembly, and voided the constitution.

Bokassa's regime was marked by unpredictability, frequent cabinet changes, and personal use of power. He ruled by decree. Political opponents were executed or given long prison terms. Many were accused of treason, arrested, or expelled. In an effort to control crime, Bokassa set harsh terms for thieves: the loss of ears and hands, among them. He ordered prison sentences for "vagabonds," "idlers," and tax evaders. No one knew what to expect next. As a result, after an early upsurge in the economy, progress came to a halt.

Central African Empire

On December 4, 1976, Bokassa proclaimed Central Africa an Empire and was crowned emperor in an elaborate ceremony costing over $25 million. He donned a crown of 2,000 diamonds, sat on a gold-plated throne, and transported his retinue in a fleet of 50 Mercedes cars. However, of 2,000 invited guests, only 400 showed up.

Becoming increasingly unstable, Bokassa personally led his troops in beatings of convicted thieves and, in 1978, was accused of taking part in the killing of 100 students who had rioted to protest an order to wear uniforms made by members of the royal family.

A government-in-exile was formed and, in September 1979, with the help of the French government and three hundred of its troops, Bokassa was overthrown in a bloodless coup while he was visiting in Libya. Former president Dacko, who had served as Bokassa's personal advisor, was returned to power and the country renamed the Central African Republic. Bokassa was granted asylum by Ivory Coast.

Dacko promised to restore democratic freedoms and called for "national unity." The country began anew its efforts to stabilize the government, restore the economy, and raise the living standard of its people.

ECONOMY

The Central African Republic is rich in natural resources. Diamond deposits are located west of Bangui and north of Bakouma. There are about 10,000 tons of uranium reserves, some iron ore, and coal. Waterfalls are a potential source of hydroelectric power. Large stands of hardwood timber grow in the rain forest and agricultural land is fertile.

There has been an attempt to develop herds of livestock and there are now 600,000 cattle, 80,000 pigs, and 560,000 sheep in the country. But the presence of the tsetse fly is a continuous threat.

Most Central Africans are farmers, producing little more than the food they eat. Production of cash crops increased, however, under a development program called "Operation Bokassa."

Coffee and cotton are the chief crops raised for export. Coffee accounts for about two-fifths of the total; cotton, diamonds, and timber, about one-fifth each. Other cash crops are cocoa, rubber, palm oil products, tobacco, bananas, and groundnuts.

Crops depend on good weather. Good weather in 1976 and 1977, combined with better organization and increased world prices, brought exports to $80 million.

Production has suffered from lack of insecticides, fertilizers, and trained personnel. Transportation and communications are poor. There is no railroad, and roads, which were once quite good, have fallen into disrepair.

CAR needs foreign aid but, except for France, other countries grew less and less willing to take a chance with Bokassa. Perhaps, with their new leadership, financial aid from abroad, and time, the CAR and its people will begin to prosper.

FOR FURTHER READING

Achebe, Chenua. *Things Fall Apart*. New York: Anchor Press, 1975.

Carpenter, Allan. *Nigeria*. Chicago: Children's Press, 1978.

Coughlin, Robert. *Tropical Africa*. New York: Time, Inc., 1962.

Glubok, Shirley, *The Art of Africa*. New York: Harper and Row, 1965.

Joseph, Joan. *Black African Empires*. New York: Franklin Watts, 1974.

Murphy, E. Jefferson. *Understanding Africa*. New York: T. Y. Crowell, 1978.

Musgrove, Margaret. *Ashanti to Zulu: African Traditions*. New York: Dial Press, 1976.

Price, Christine. *Made in West Africa*. New York: E. P. Dutton, 1975.

Thomas, Benjamin E., Allen, William D., and Jennings, Jerry E. *Man in Africa*. Grand Rapids: The Fideler Co., 1972.

INDEX

Hausa, 5, 14–15, 16, 24, 25, 28
Health, 30–32, 46, 53, 59–60

Ibadan, 14, 17, 33
Ibidio, 20
Ibo, 10, 19–21, 28, 44
Ife, 5, 17, 25
Ijaw, 20

Kanem-Bornu, 5, 24, 48
Kano, 14–15
Kanuri, 20
Kom, 52

Lagos, 12–14, 17, 20, 27, 28, 32
Lake Chad, 5, 11, 24, 37, 46
Lander, Richard and John, 26
Language, 21, 45
Livingston, David, 7

Mandjia, 57
M'Baka, 56–57
Mohammed, Murtala Ramat, 28–29
Mount Cameroon, 37, 38, 40, 41, 48

Niger River, 5, 7, 12, 26
Nigeria, 6, 8, 9–35
Nok, 24, 33

Obasanjo, Olusegun, 29
Oil, 9, 29, 30
Oyo, 17, 25

Park, Mungo, 7, 26
Portuguese, 3, 4, 25, 48
Pygmies, 2, 44–45, 48, 57

Religion, 3, 7, 10, 14, 15–16, 17, 21–24, 45

Sahara, the, 1–3
Sanaga River, 38
Sara, 57
Shagari, Alhaji Shehu, 29
Shari River, 55
Soyinka, Wole, 35
Stanley, Henry Morton, 7
Sudan(ese), 5, 57

Tiv, 20
Tutuola, Amos, 35

Ubangi River, 55, 56–57

Victoria, 49

Wildlife, 41, 55–56
Wouri River, 38, 48

Yaounde, 45, 48
Yimbi, 58
Yoruba, 5, 17–18, 21, 25

Zaire, 57
Zaire River, 3, 55